MATH-Magical ABC's

$$2+2=4$$

$$\pi$$

$$\times$$

CHRISTIAN
THE MATH KID

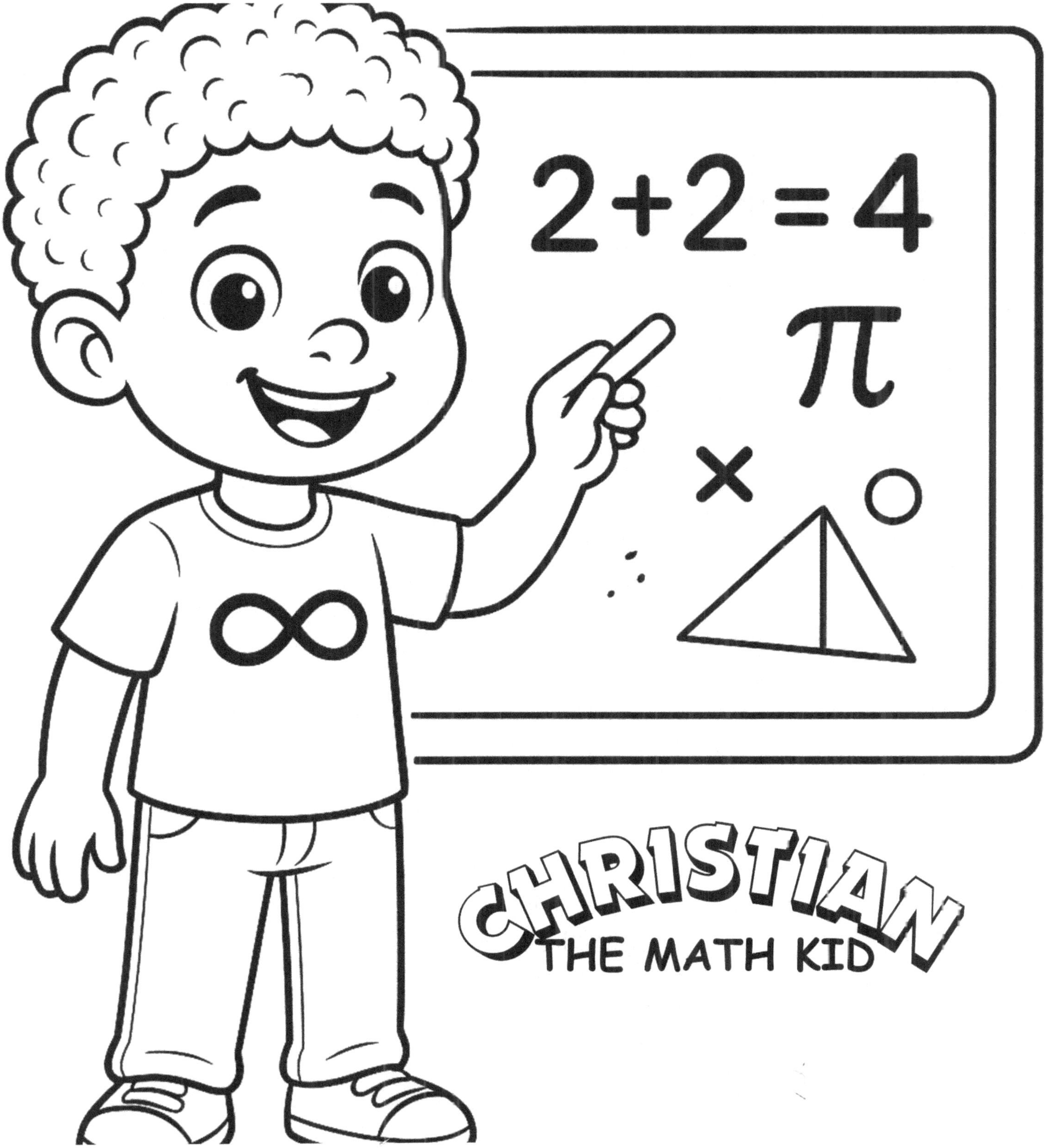

First Edition: AUGUST 2025

ISBN (Paperback): 979-8-9912311-9-0

Permission or Bulk Ordering requests should be addressed in writing to:
Takhia Gaither
The Ready Write-Her
info@thereadywriteher.com
SUBJECT: MATH ABC's Coloring Book

ABACUS

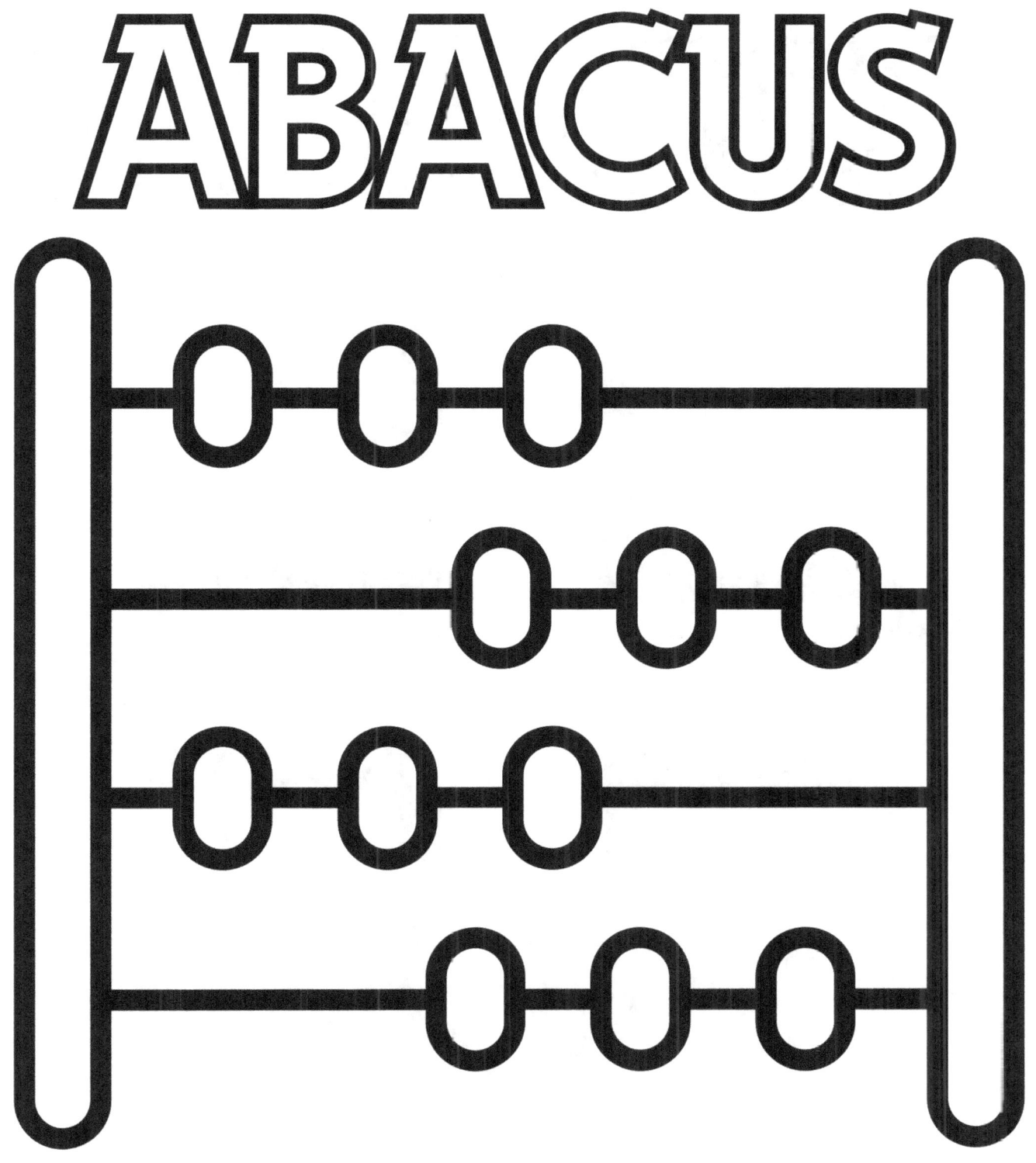

An abacus is a tool that helps you count, add, and subtract using beads that slide on rods or strings. It was used before people had calculators or computers. Each row of beads stands for a different place value like ones, tens, and hundreds.

ADDITION

Addition is when you put things together to find the total. The symbol we use is called a plus sign. It looks like a "t."

BRACKETS

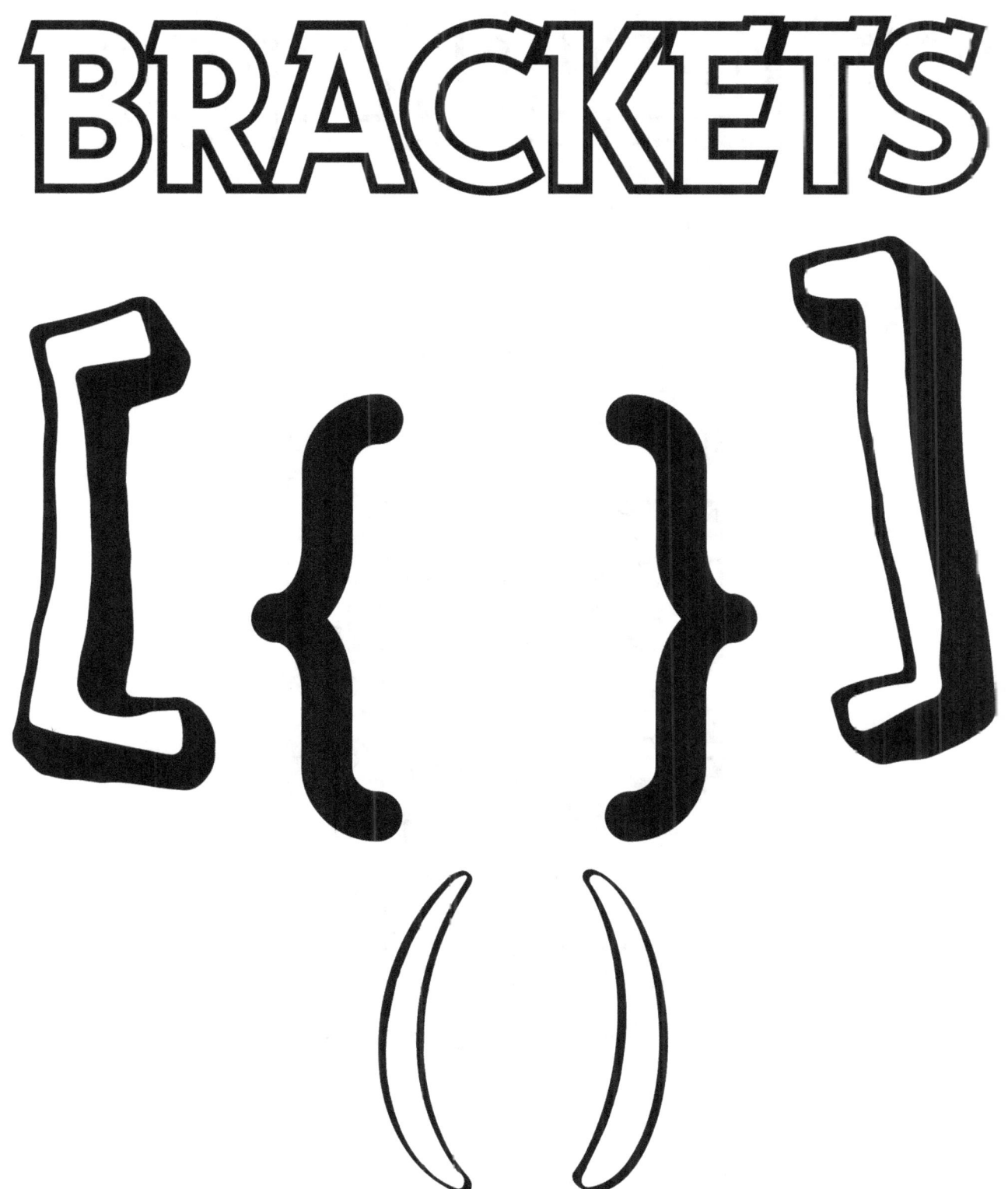

Brackets are used in mathematics to separate parts of a problem. You may see square brackets, curly braces/brackets, or parentheses. They are sometimes called grouping symbols.

CALCULATOR

Calculators are electronic tools we can use to help us solve math problems. They will do the work adding, subtracting, multiplying, and more when we input the information. They are used to save time, check our work done by hand, or for numbers that are too big and complicated to do operations by hand.

DIVISION

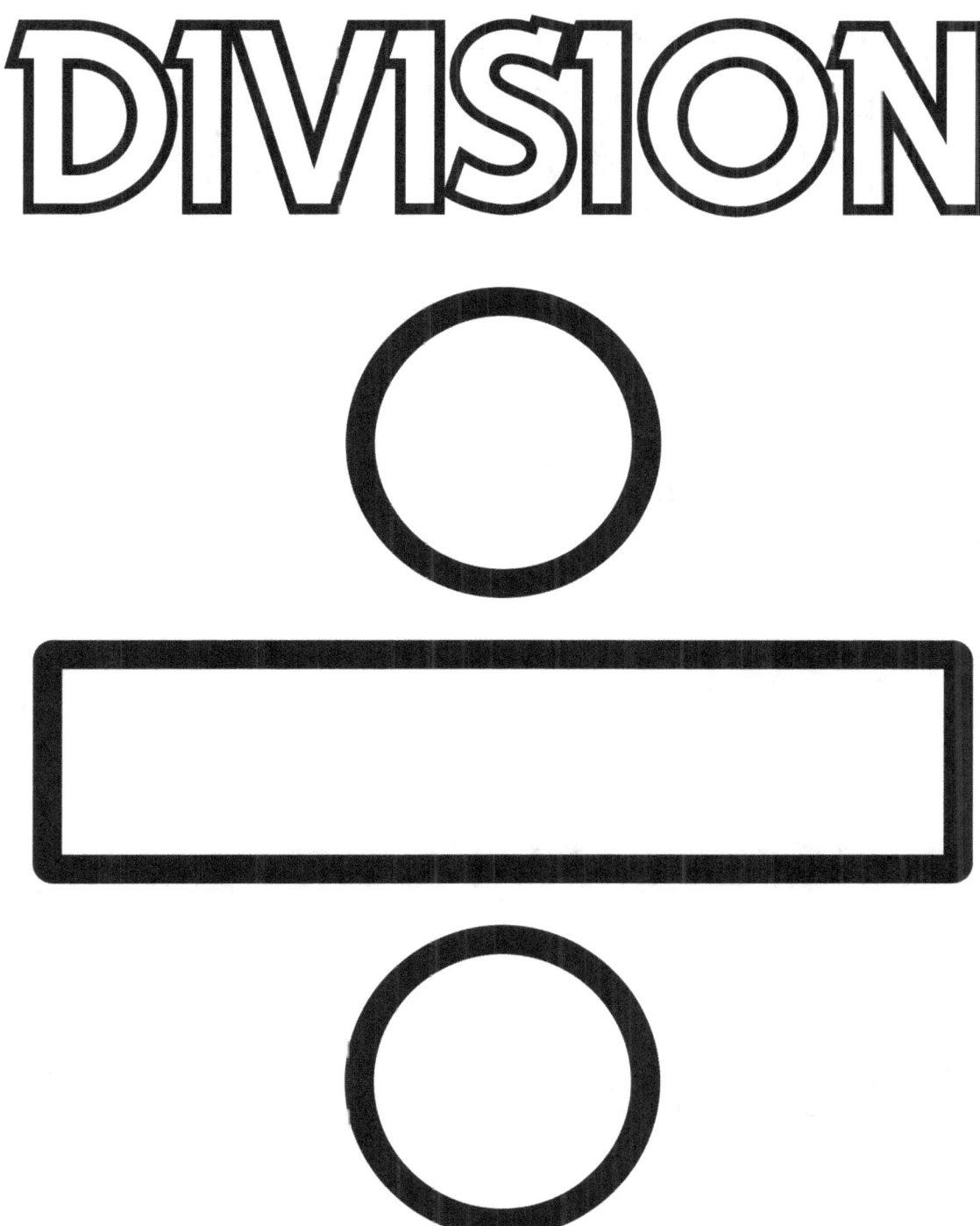

Division is the mathematical operation that allows us to split things in equal parts.

EQUAL

Equal (eaual to) is the symbol used when two numbers, equations, or quantities are the same.

FRACTION

Fractions represent the part of a whole. They written as the top number (numerator), straight or slanted bar, the bottom number (denominator). You say it as 1 over 2.

GREATER THAN

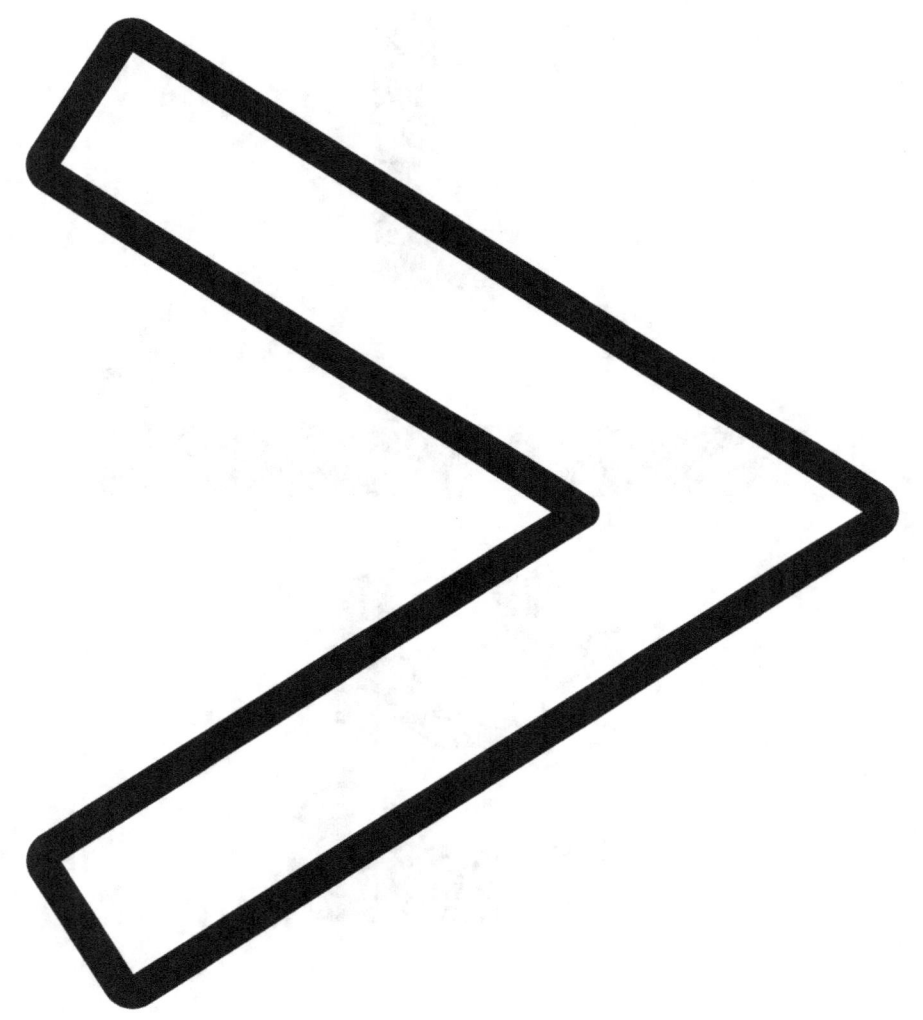

Greater than is the symbol used to represent one quantity being greater than another.

HEXAGON

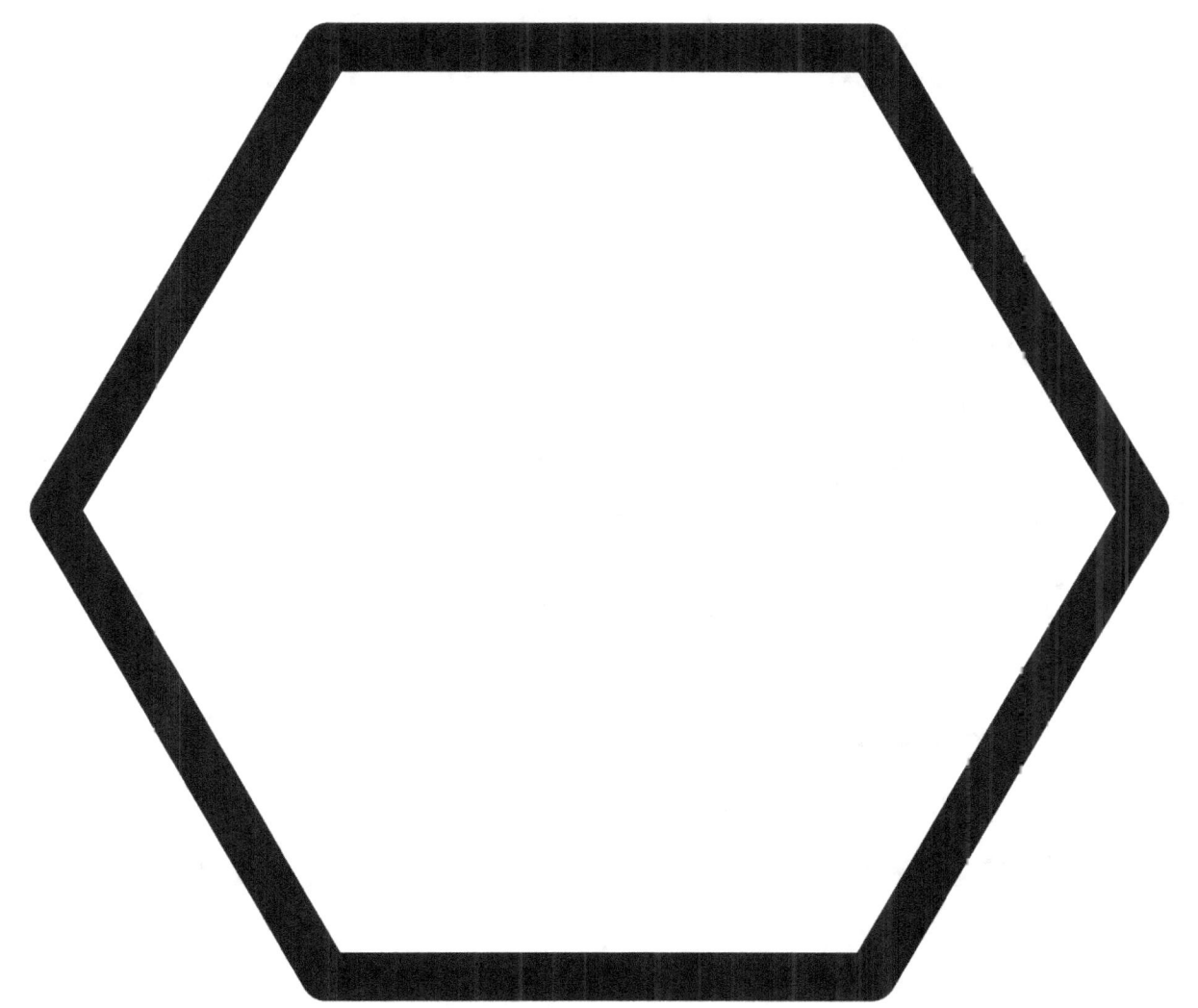

Hexagon is a 6-sided shape. Each angle inside the hexagon is 120 degrees. The total is 720 degrees. All of the sides may not be equal.

INFINITY

Infinity is something that never ends. It s a number that keeps going on forever. The symbol we use to represent it is a sideways 8.

JUMP STRATEGY

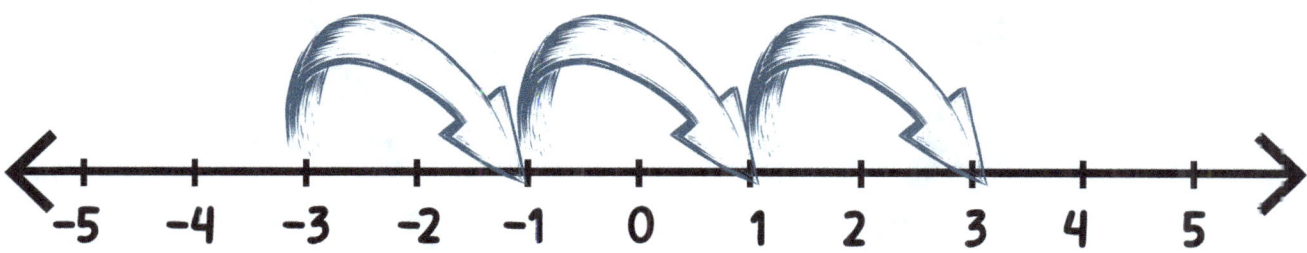

The Jump Strategy is used on a number line to help you add or subtract. You pick the starting point and then move to the right for addition the number of spaces it tells you or the left for subtraction problems.

KITE

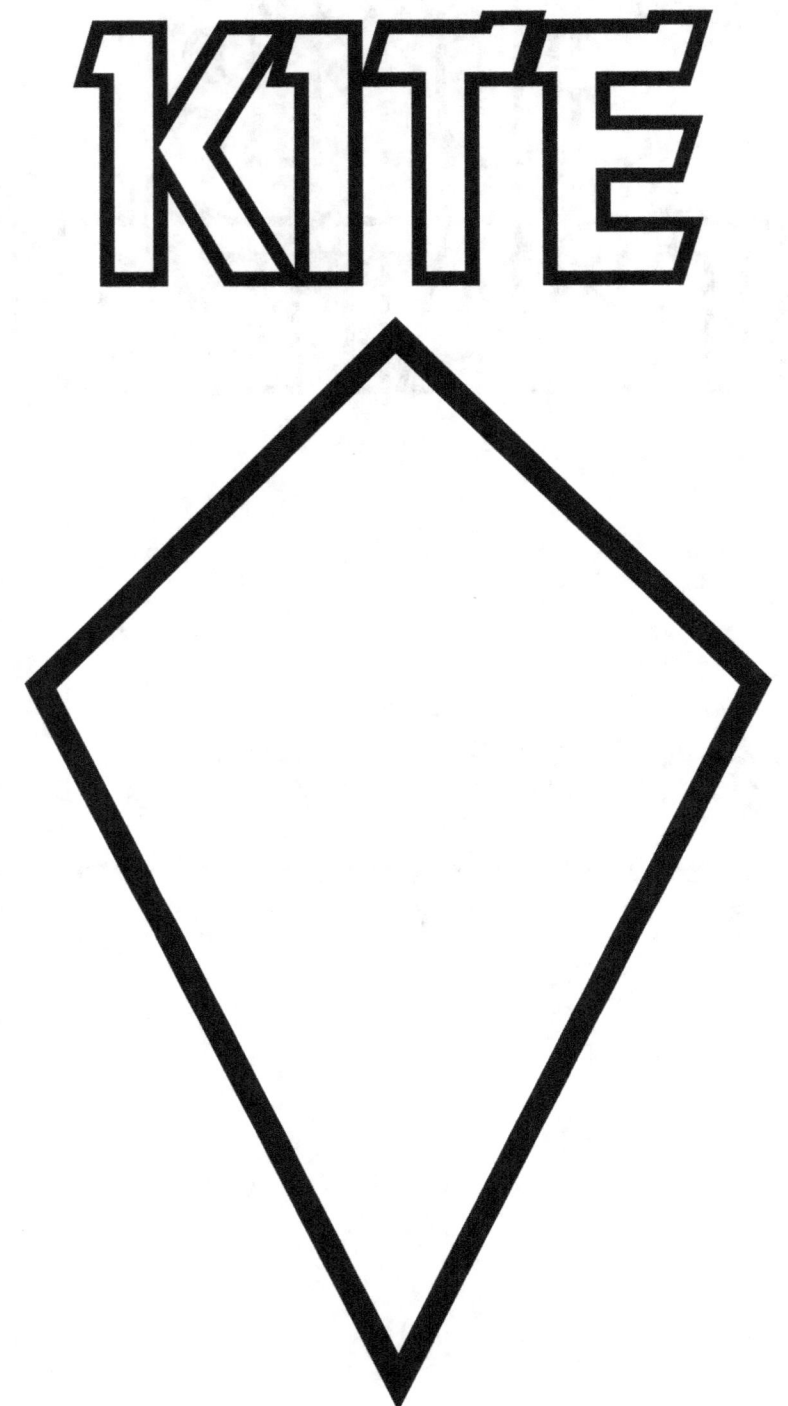

A kite shape is a four-sided shape that has two pairs of adjacent sides that are conguent. The diagonals of the kite intersect at right angles and the diagonal is a line of symmetry.

LESS THAN

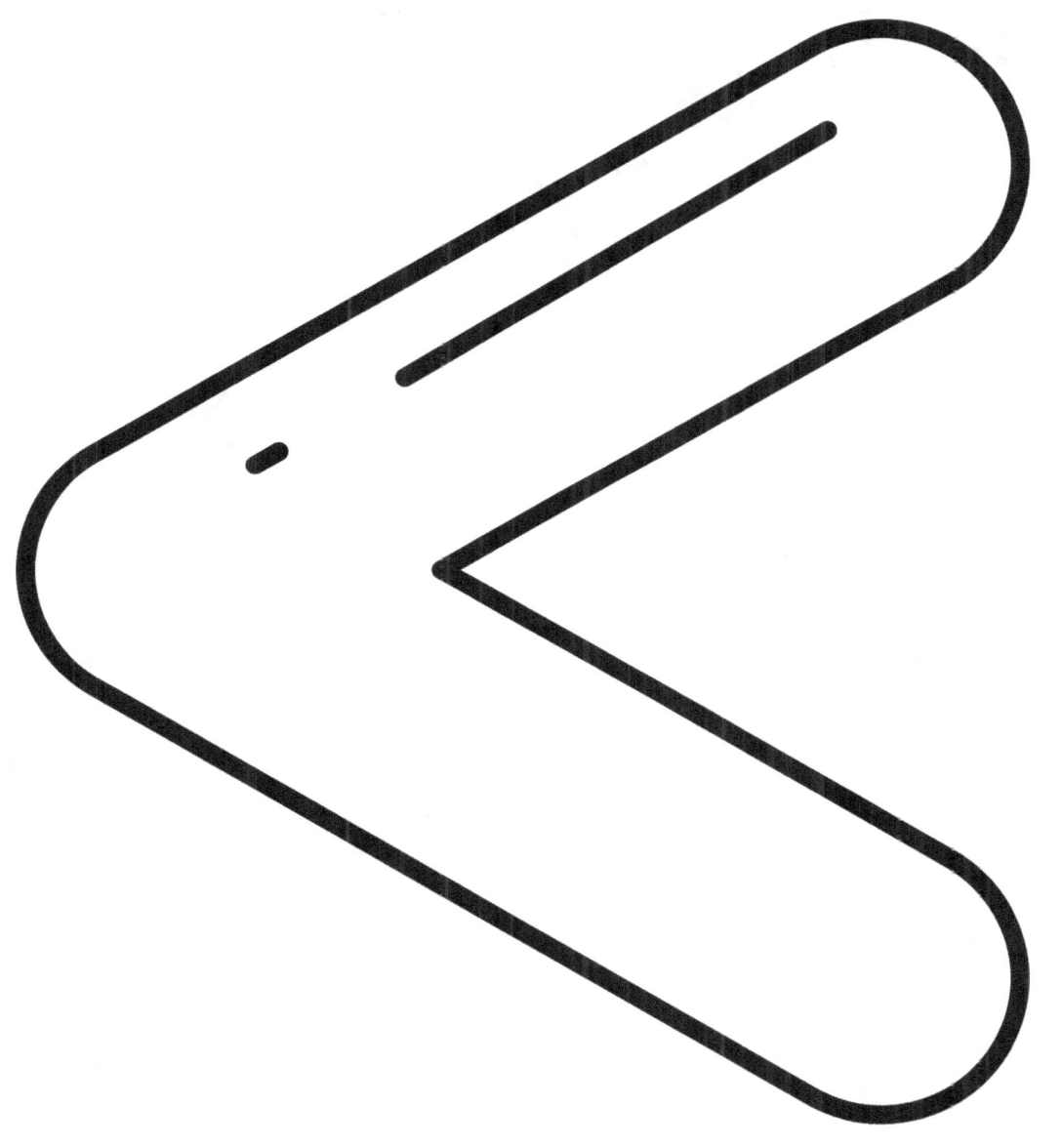

Less than tells us when one number or quantity is smaller than the other.

MULTIPLICATION

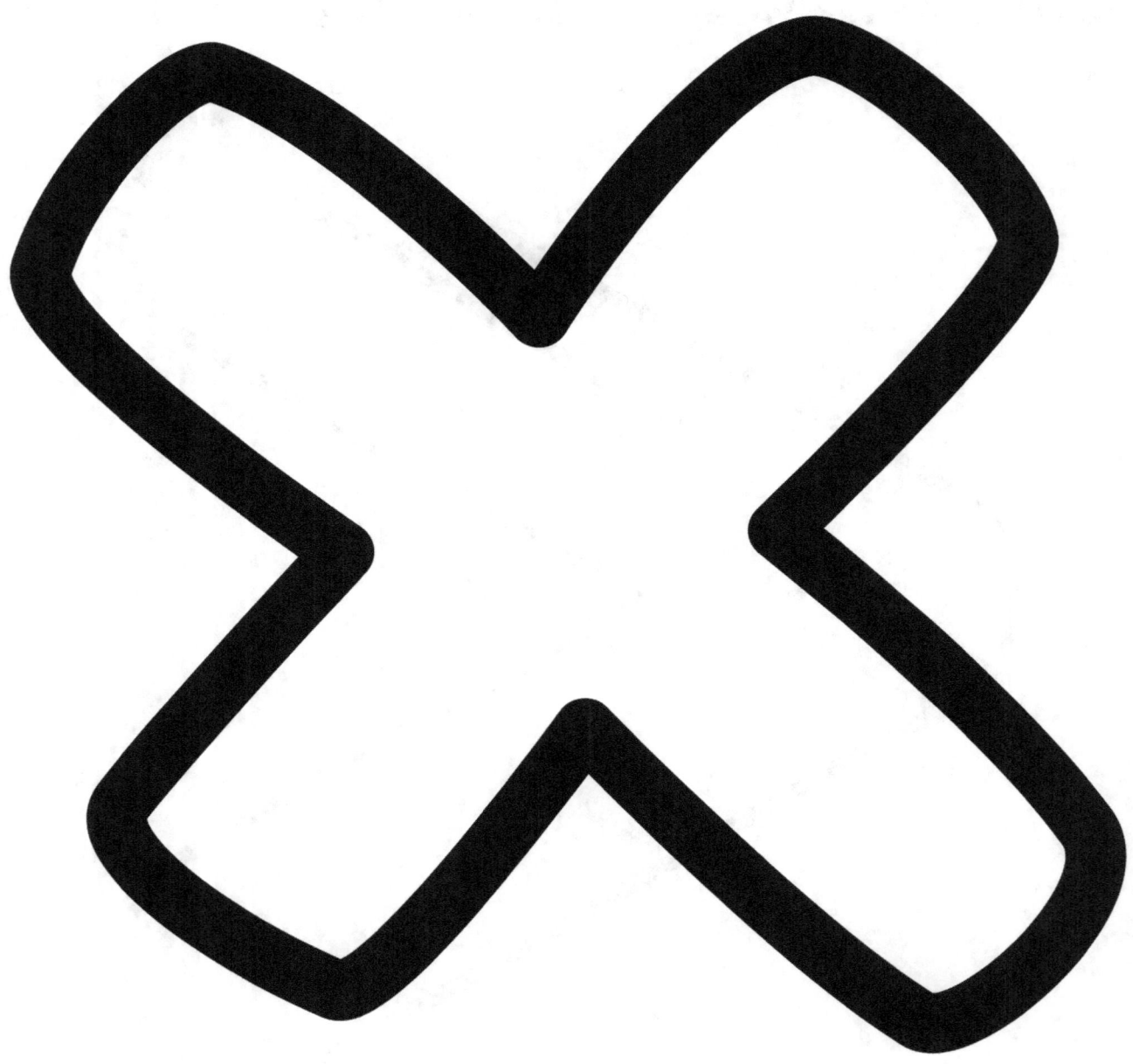

Multiplication is a fast way to add the same number repeatedly. It is usually symbolized by an x. 2 x 3 = 6 is read 2 times 2 equals 6 it means add two, three times and the answer is 6.

NUMERATOR

A numerator is the top number in a fraction.

OCTAGON

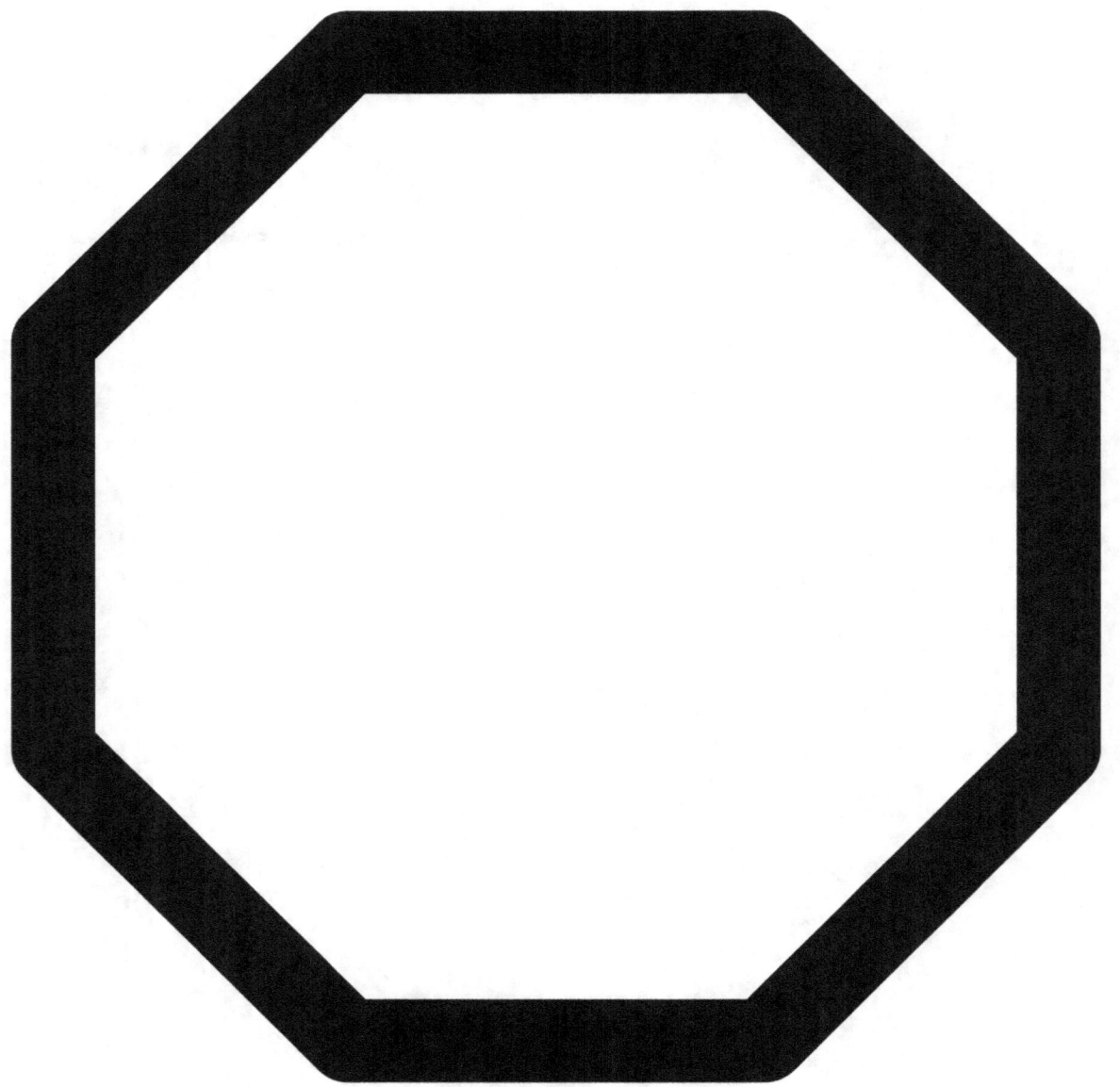

An octagon is an 8-sided figure. All of the angles of an octagon measure 135 degrees and all of the sides will be be equal lengths.

PENTAGON

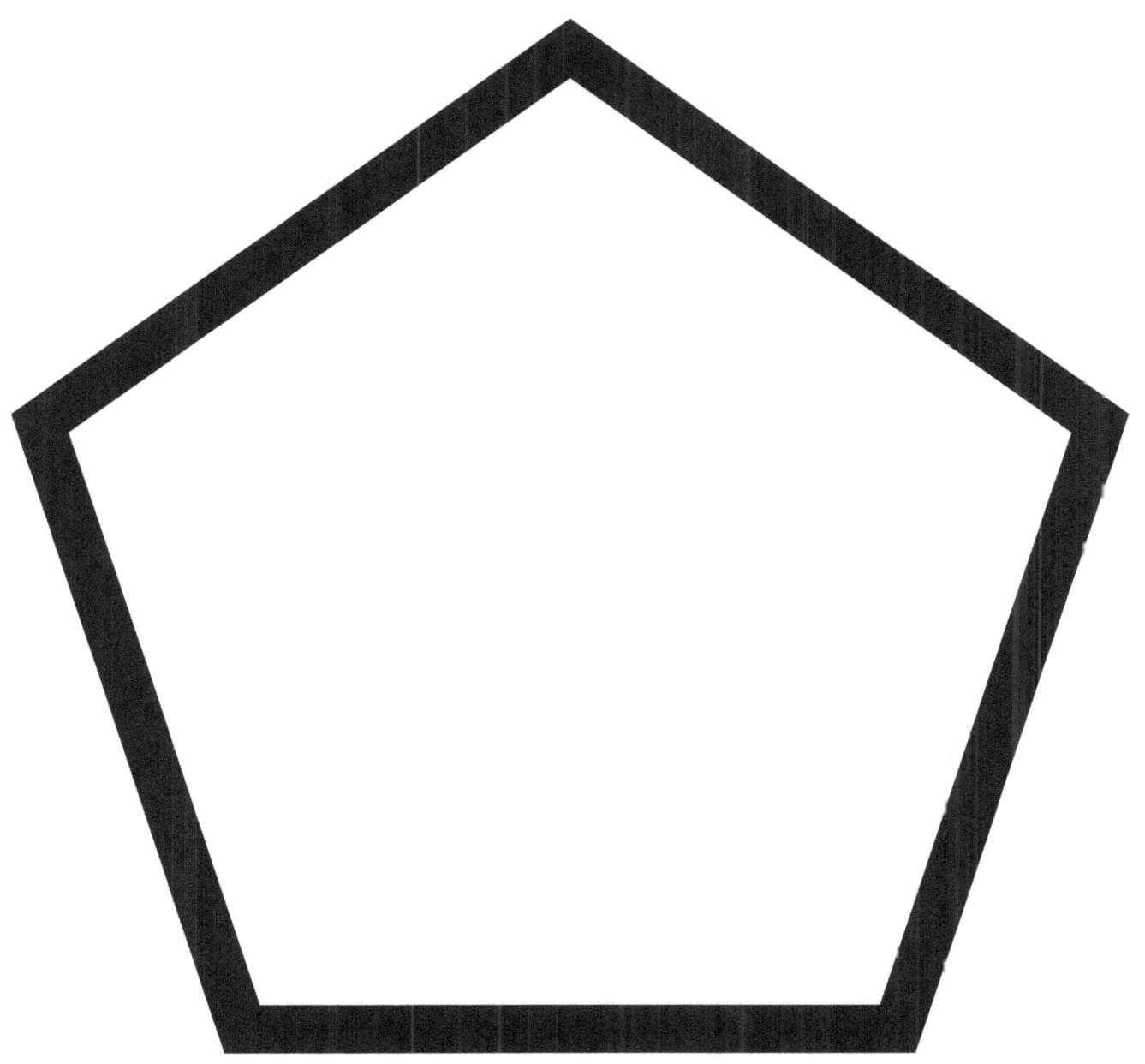

A pentagon is a five-sided figure with 5 equal side lengths and 5 equal angles. The angels measure 108 degrees each for a total of 540 degrees.

QUOTIENT

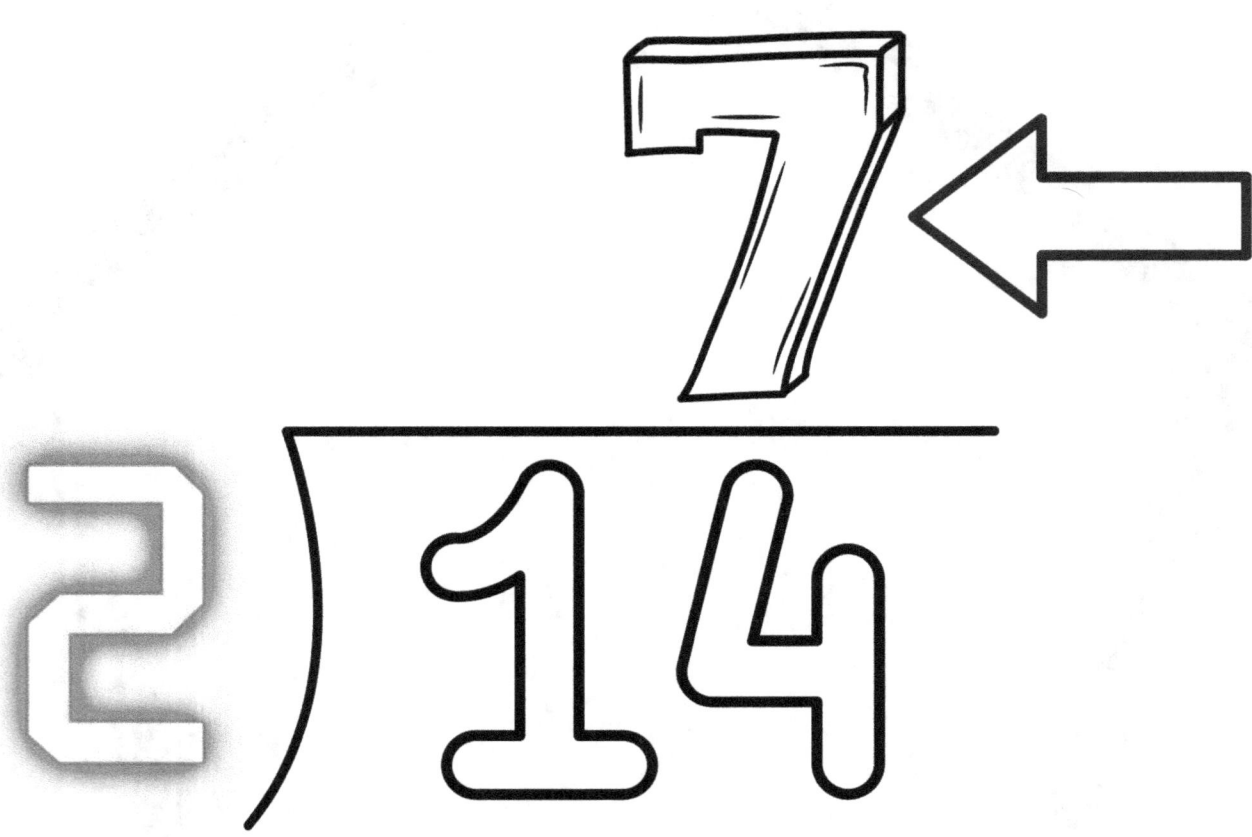

The quotient is the answer to a division problem.

RADIUS

The radius is half the distance across a circle. It is symbolized by "r."

SPHERE

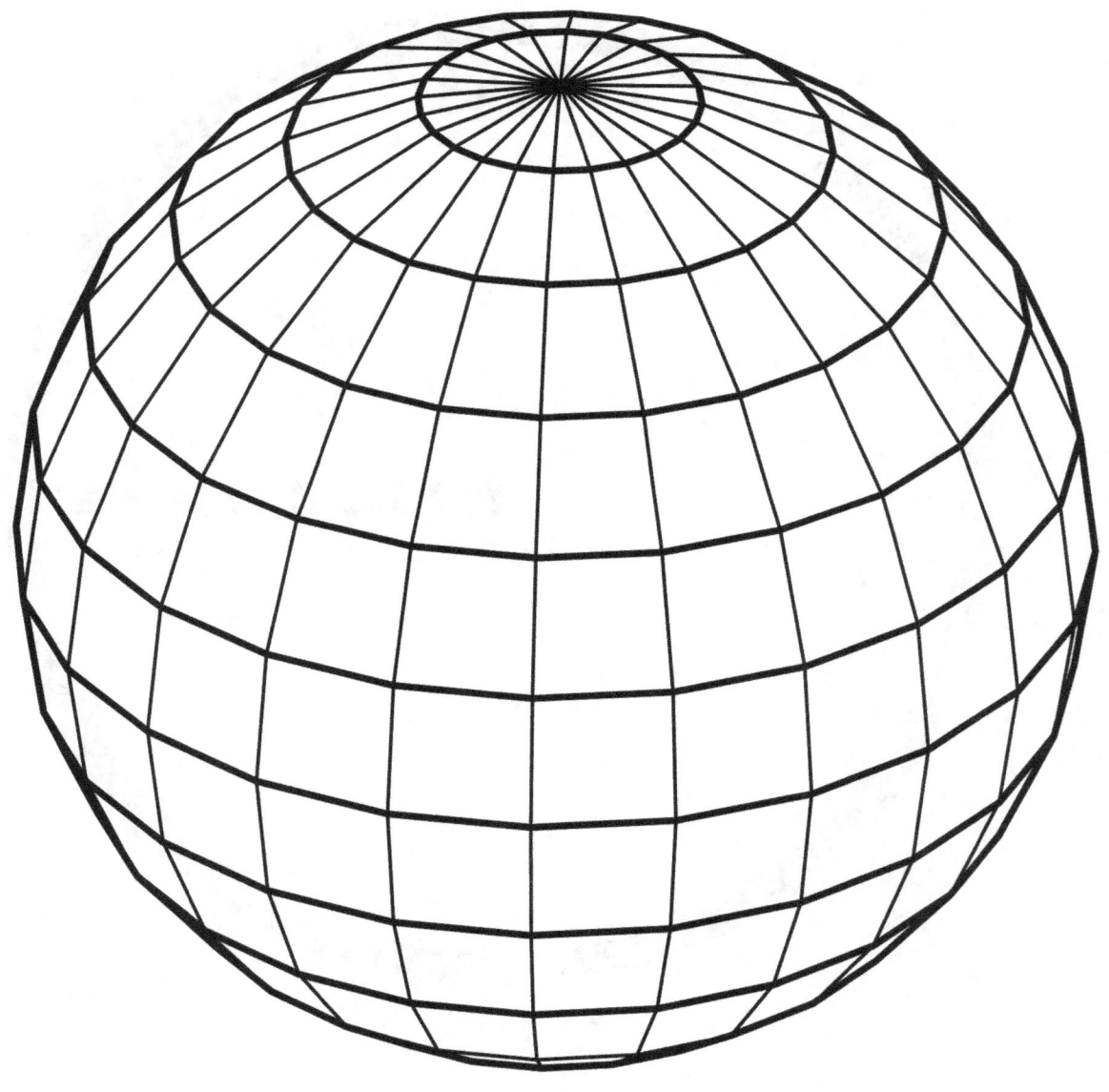

A sphere is a 3-dimensional circle. Some examples of spheres are basketballs, globes,

SUBTRACTION

Subtraction is when you take things away from a total. The symbol we use to show subtraction is called a minus sign.

TRIANGLE

A triangle is a 3-sided shaped. The sum of the angles in a triangle always add up to 180 degrees. The sides do not have to always be equal.

UNKNOWN

$$3 + ? = 11$$

The unknown is a missing number in a math problem that you have to figure out. Sometimes you'll see a blank space with or without a question mark in to represent the unknown. Other times you'll seen just a question mark.

VARIABLE

$$3 + X = 11$$

A variable is a letter used to represent an unknown in a mathematics equation.

WIDTH

The width is how wide something is from side to side. It is symbolized by the letter "w."

X-AXIS

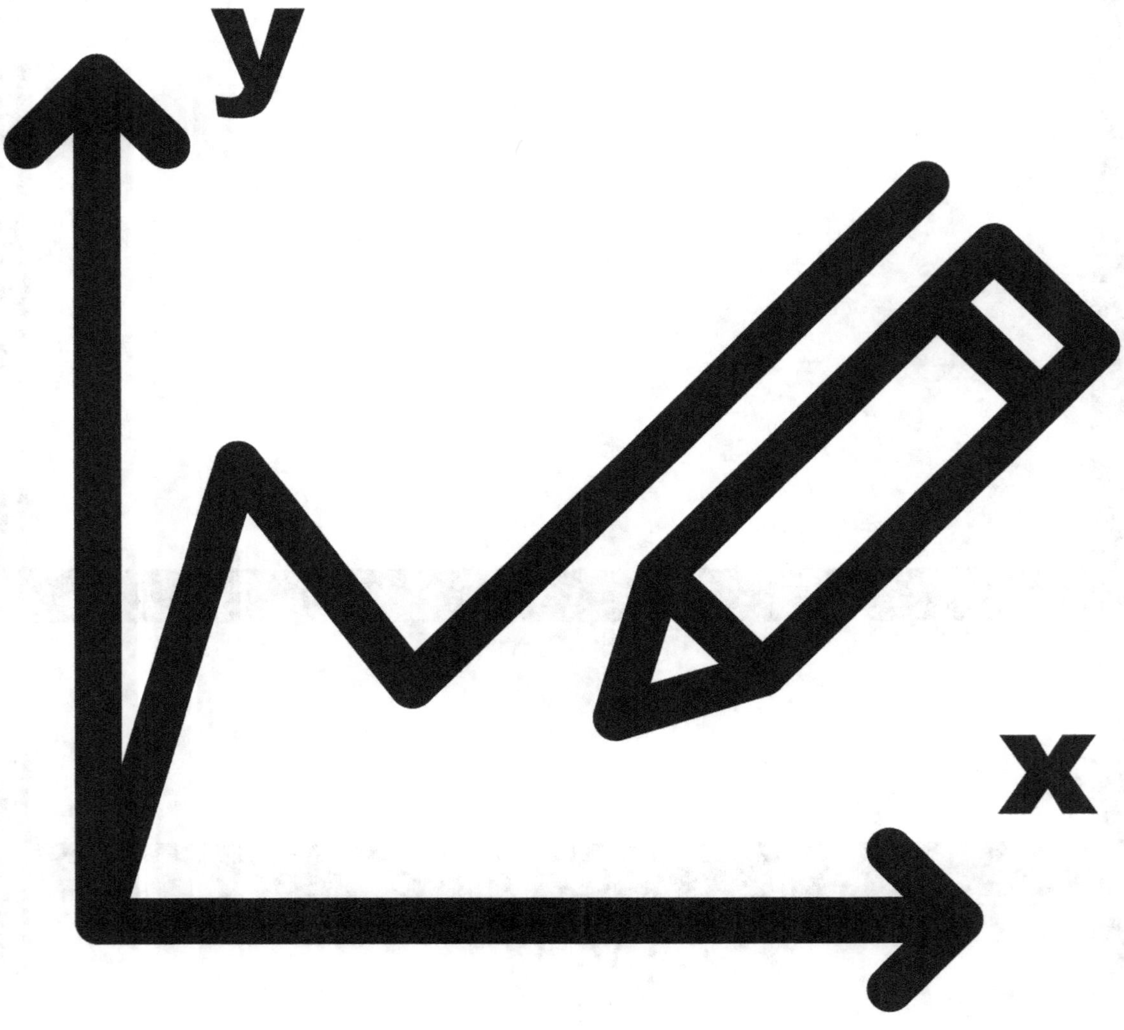

The x-axis goes across (from left to right) on a graph or coordinate plane.

Y-AXIS

The y-axis goes up and down on a graph or coordinate plane.

ZERO

Zero is the number that represents having none of something.

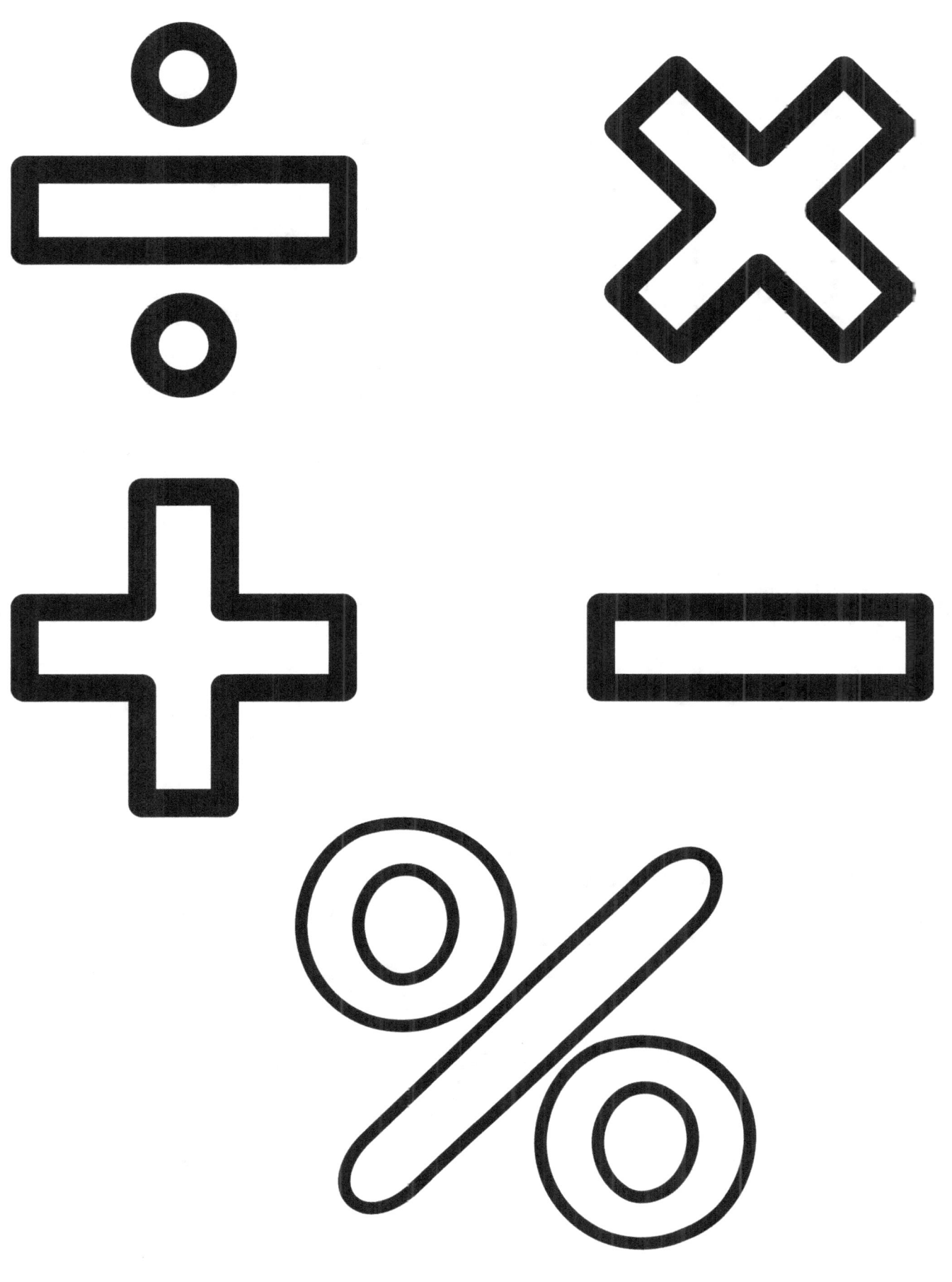

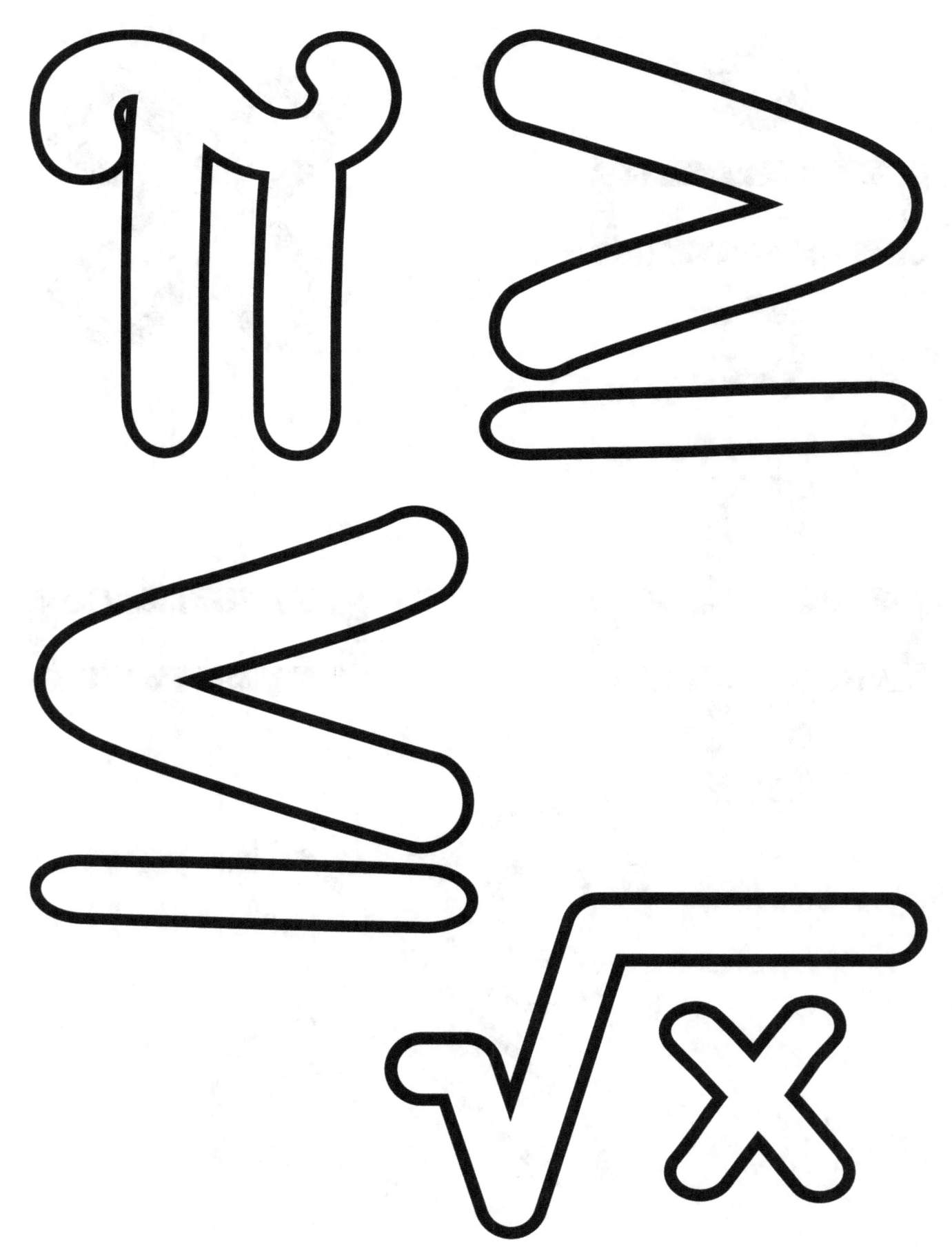

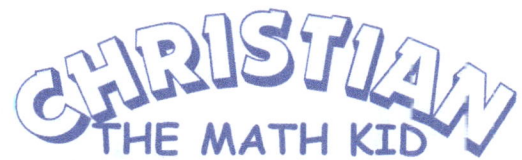

CHRISTIAN
THE MATH KID

Be the first to know when the next Christian the Math Kid adventure begins! SCAN BELOW!

Thank you!

Christian the Math Kid
&
Takhia the Teacher

www.ingramcontent.com/pod-product-compliance
Lightning Source LLC
Chambersburg PA
CBHW080812120626

46556CB00009B/3302